SCALE MODEL OF A COUNTRY AT DAWN

JOHN SIBLEY WILLIAMS

SCALE MODEL OF A COUNTRY AT DAWN

Cider Press Review
San Diego

Cider Press Review
PO BOX 33384
San Diego, CA, USA
ciderpressreview.com

First edition
10 9 8 7 6 5 4 3 2 1 0

ISBN: 978-1-930781-60-3
Library of Congress Control Number: 2021941914
Cover illustration by Hagar Vardimon
Author photograph by Staci Michelle Williams
Book design by Caron Andregg

Winner of the 2020 Cider Press Review Book Award
ciderpressreview.com/bookaward.

Printed in the United States of America
at Bookmobile in Minneapolis, MN USA.

Acknowledgements

American Poetry Journal: The Gift and Restoration

Apricity Press: All We Ever Wanted Was Everything

Arts & Letters: Solar Retinopathy (Finalist for the Rumi Prize in Poetry)

Balkan Press: Our Pasts, Like Lighthouses

Baltimore Review: Self-Portrait as Travelogue

Basalt: Some of What Sings

Bayou Magazine: Conch

Bellingham Review: Imprint and Aperture

Blueline: Bifurcation

Broad River Review: Sinkholes (Finalist for the Rash Award)

Cascadia Magazine: Appaloosa

Catamaran Literary Reader: Prayer for the Boy Lost Inside the Boy

The Columbia Review: Object Permanence

The Comstock Review: A Careful Study: Postmortem (Finalist for the Muriel Craft Bailey Memorial Award)

Everyman Library Anthology (Knopf): Suture (reprint) and Sediment (reprint)

The Fourth River: Wide as a Heaven Hemmed in by Hills

Free Verse: A Journal of Contemporary Poetry & Poetics: We Carry Wildfires in Our Guts

GASHER: Being Islands

Gulf Coast: Harborless

Harpur Palate: Enter // Exit

Hotel Amerika: Coat of Bees

Isthmus: Sediment

Lake Effect: Square Dance at Dusk

Lumina: Orbit // Obit

The Madison Review: Like a plague of locusts (Winner of the Phyllis Smart-Young Prize)

Manzano Mountain Review: Self-Portrait as My Mother as a Cliff Face

The Meadow: The Confession

The Minnesota Review: Community Service

The New Guard: Backyard Hymnal (Finalist for Knightville Poetry Contest)

New Reader Magazine: Nativity

North American Review: Echolocation

North Dakota Quarterly: Portrait of a Portrait on Fire, Canaveral, and American Bounty

Passages North: Interlude

Poetry South: Oasis

Poetry Super Highway: Leave No Trace

Prairie Schooner: Sycamores

Puerto del Sol: All the names of all the men

Raleigh Review: Ordinary Beasts, Fever, Synonyms for Paradise, and Forever Daylight (Winner of the Laux/Millar Poetry Prize)

River Heron Review: Genesis

Rivet: Where Astrology Ends

Salamander: Parallax

Santa Clara Review: Carcinogen, Larynx, and On This Night, or Any Other

Small Orange: Winter Bazaar

The Sewanee Review: Controlled Burn

Solstice: The Gospel According to Here

The Southern Review: Oncology

Sow's Ear Review: Property Line (Finalist for the Sow's Ear Poetry Review Contest)

Sugar House Review: Zoo Animals and Reading *Ozymandias* in Astoria

Third Coast: In the Language of Drought

TriQuarterly: The whole I'm told we return to

Up North Lit: Everywhere is the same and Open Season (Finalist for the Up North Poetry Prize)

Western Humanities Review: As It Is on Earth and Apiary & Woodshop

Wild Gods: The Ecstatic in Contemporary Poetry and Lyric Prose (New Rivers Press anthology): Prayer for the Boy Lost Inside the Boy (reprint) and Aperture (reprint)

Willow Springs: Suture

The Worcester Review: Ministry

Yemassee: Scale Model of a Country at Dawn

ZYZZYVA: Salinas

Contents

Acknowledgements / vii

The Gift / xiii

❦ ORDINARY BEASTS ❦

Ordinary Beasts / 3
Orbit // Obit / 4
Synonyms for Paradise / 5
Like a plague of locusts / 6
Harborless / 7
Self-Portrait as My Mother as a Cliff Face / 8
Enter // Exit / 9
Imprint / 10
Carcinogen / 11
Oncology / 13
A Careful Study: Postmortem / 14
All the names of all the men / 16
Scale Model of a Country at Dawn / 17
Property Line / 18
Where Astrology Ends / 19
Nativity / 21
On This Night, or Any Other / 22
Appaloosa / 23
Prayer for the Boy Lost Inside the Boy / 24
As It Is on Earth / 26
Larynx / 27
Some of What Sings / 28
Conch / 29
Our Pasts, Like Lighthouses / 30

❦ Suture ❦

All We Ever Wanted Was Everything / 35

Everywhere is the same   / 36
Sinkholes   / 37
Solar Retinopathy   / 38
Self-Portrait as Travelogue   / 39
Ministry   / 40
Apiary & Woodshop   / 41
Coat of Bees   / 42
Community Service   / 43
Open Season   / 44
Winter Bazaar   / 46
Backyard Hymnal   / 47
Portrait of a Portrait on Fire   / 48
Leave No Trace   / 49
We Carry Wildfires in Our Guts   / 51
In the Language of Drought   / 52
Oasis   / 53
Zoo Animals   / 54
Fever   / 55
Sycamores   / 56
Echolocation   / 57
Suture   / 58

☙ Object Permanence ❧

The Gospel According to Here   / 63
Parallax   / 64
Forever Daylight   / 65
Square Dance at Dusk   / 66
Reading *Ozymandias* in Astoria   / 67
Controlled Burn   / 68
Interlude   / 69
Wide as a Heaven Hemmed in by Hills   / 70
Canaveral   / 71
Genesis   / 72
Sediment   / 73
Bifurcation   / 74
Aperture   / 75

The whole I'm told we return to   / 76
American Bounty   / 77
The Confession   / 78
Restoration   / 79
Salinas   / 80
Object Permanence   / 81

Being Islands   / 85

The Gift

Tonight I will make something for you
not of jawbone & break & the usual

starlessness, not idled by half-meant
promise, a hammer handed down without

nails or wood to drive them through,
a childhood missing one or more parents:

something the light must struggle to enter.
I swear I won't kill anything to make it

durable; this time what lasts will last
despite me. The light will be its own.

The angles as true as I'm able to sand them.
No grief attached. No salvation or need for it.

Just a rough little box built from my bones
to keep the bones you'll collect in.

Ordinary Beasts

Ordinary Beasts

There are worse ways to die.
   The tin foil sword my son hacks off the heads

of hydrangeas with, turned inward. The poisoned
   teacup my daughter serves to the stuffed bear

clutching a fat pink heart I gave her
   for her third birthday. The sky

peeling back layer after layer like an onion,
   a bedsheet in August, & the world

warms. It's amazing
   what you can find beneath

what you're looking for. Beneath the doe
   we left for dead, a mangle of maggots

gleaming white & true. Beneath me,
   my son pinned to the earth

giggling as if the moment belongs to us.
   I once made a necklace of paperclips

& wore it like a string of enemies' ears. Even if I knew
   how to take it off, I wouldn't. I haven't.

We all need something to scream into. Void.
   Mirror. It'd be a shame to mourn ourselves alone.

Orbit // Obit

—for Tishani Doshi, after a friend's suicide

Our drawing stars
together into brand new constellations
named after monsters & angry father
figures in the margins of unread textbooks

hasn't changed the trajectory.

Snow still stacks like bodies. Above,
clouds cotton & disband. Last night
I heard a dog in the valley wound heaven
with a single wail. It was the sound of men

rubbing themselves against the world,
claiming ownership of what cannot be
owned. I wish you were still here to
bear the brunt of night's blow.
                                    Instead

the light struggling through these disrobed
trees hurts like a given-up-on century, like
bruised apples sinking deeper into winter,

like watching you trace a star's path
with what would become your trigger finger
back and forth across a brilliantly
                                    vanquished sky.

Synonyms for Paradise

I'd like to start again. Instead of
a car that won't start & this parody of sky,
a working engine, gas, a crisp blue forgettable
morning. Instead of that same old forever,

a temporary heaven of breath & sex & pain
& verbs. The children it's too late to have,
let's have them. The chapter where my mother
starts calling me by her father's name: expunged.

If owning a thing erases it, I'd like to start
by buying up all the homes I've ever lived in.
Then everywhere I'll never plant roots.
It hurts me to do it, but let's let the synonyms

for *joy* & for *grief* bleed together, like salt
& fresh water, like poles of a magnet.
That we all die before we're finished
is no excuse to abandon this worn-out

car by the side of some nameless road,
flipped over, only partially on fire.
That we should know when we see it
is not the same thing as a promise.

Like a plague of locusts

or chaff erupting from split wheat,
though if I were in the storm's path—

practicing my dying or unburying
my daughter from our wind-wracked

house just to bury her again in an equally
unforgiving earth—I'm sure no metaphor

would suffice. This is not the sky
our grandmothers taught us to pray to;

this canvas of bald trees & splintered
schools not like anything

we can shape a childhood from.
Harvey, Irma, Maria. The intimacy

of naming without knowing. I don't know
where the line is between empathy

& the world. I imagine the revolver of her
tiny body misfiring over and over into

a savage wind. A darkness so dark it hurts
to see the other side through it.

Harborless

If I had known, I would have tested
the rope for strain & pull. I would have
scraped the salt from its weakening mast,
layered resin & fiberglass, plugged each hole.

If I had known all boats eventually yield
to the current, I would have readied myself
long ago—as a youth, or before that, a son
still sucking sea-spit from stones & casting

them back, as if there's a going back after
you've held something in your mouth long
enough to taste. & lose. I would have asked
different questions—ones with answers.

I would have believed my father
when he said you can't drink saltwater
& so all oceans are thirsty. I would
have let that statement wound me.

That old detonation of autumn—its brilliant
scattering, its violent crimson breaking up
the trees into green & gone, its storms.
A better boy; I would have sat on the peer

all night, every night, like my mother, dress
wet up to her knees, fingers a loosening
cathedral. I would have stowed away beneath
my bed—a kind of prayer that's not a prayer at all.

Self-Portrait as My Mother as a Cliff Face

Eyes: gray smudges on a hard
gray swatch: shale & striations,

moss, a few swallows building
nests from mud & plummet.

Even here, ankle-deep in stars
prayed to & stars abandoned

for a brightness that can be
passed openly between palms

like an Indian Head nickel or
matchstick or urn, I forget silence

is the source of all echoes, home
the high-water stain on that cliff

where all suicides are too briefly gods.
It doesn't take long for water

to find an escape route or us
to lean our flames against a wall

of infinities or infinity to lose
patience & drown itself in promise.

It's true: the ocean is set on repeat.
Equally true: this vastness between

masses of land turned out to be just
another door thrown wide as a mouth,

                    both entrance & exit.

Enter // Exit

Still wet with yesterday's
salt & spit, the stilts
meant to keep us anchored
safely above the sea
are bowing. The wood
smells like a rain bucket
unemptied all season.
The crossbeams, an unwanted
green. Even the gulls refuse
our crusts, our open palms,
as if blaming us for wanting
to live so far above the surface.
But even this sag & lean
is temporary, we remind
ourselves. One of these days
we'll crumble, drown, or
learn to hold each other
up, renovate. I don't think
I trust gravity as much
as I used to. More & more,
we're fearing our foundation, that
blue eternity roiling beneath.
& in the next room, wailing
from their cradles, a pair of
prologues already beginning
to enter the narrative.

We don't have the heart yet
to tell them how much heart
it takes to remain its subject.

Imprint

There are some people who leave impressions not so lasting
as the imprint of an oar upon the water.
— *Kate Chopin*

For example: breath. For example: a father.
   Or dawn chewing up fireflies, raking the stars

down to campfire ash. The child you'll spend longer
   grieving than raising, the sea's

clumsy mirror, the churchlessness of raw earth.
   For example: that inevitable

first footprint sunk into the riverclay of an un-
   mapped country. Heaven or hell or just another

Sunday wandering the wild outskirts of a fenceless
   field. How everything is entirely unknowable

until ripped from the earth & tasted. Spit back, sometimes
   swallowed. I'm done trying to breathe

life back into imaginary dead things. My hands, for example.
   How much more you must have expected from them.

Carcinogen

Lately, an infertile valley. An old war-
damaged church. Naught, as in

the lungs can't hold it all in
anymore. Breath, as in a fawn

scraping her dry tongue raw
on red arroyo sands. The bullet

another's hunger pushes deep
into her hide. A mother

who tries to inhale the world
away, porchside, pluming

like the smokestacks dad
says define (as in not

disrupt, beautify
maybe) this

afterthought of horizon.
To fail,

is what I mean,
at owning one's face.

As in *tell me everything*
you need to ruin to make

a body livable again. To live in it,
lately, after its ruin (steeple

snapped off, this hollowed
fist of land unclenching,

deer skin stretched over
the mantle, all one's violences

contained in a single cell, finally,
spreading). As in the birds

drawing their arrows back. Fire. *Fire.*
The air, I mean. That sting.

Oncology

Ward: as in division of;

as in a neighborhood
carved from the body
of a city; as in a child

raised by childless
parents or some great
aunt he's never met
yet is told to hold
in his heart like a mother;

as in care or custody's
lost agency;

as in the wide-open space
within a castle's walls where
life is meant to go on

despite the world
wearing down the gate;

as in the part of a lock
that keeps the wrong key
from turning, a malignancy

from entering; & when it does
despite all the synonyms for prayer
read over her deathbed:

averting, repelling, resisting;

as in after everything excised
how much more there is left to lose.

A Careful Study: Postmortem

No matter how
                many pins hold it down,

the wings
              tremble; in your mind

still attempting flutter,
                    flight, like

any child, terrified
                  every body

is part yours; even this
                  strange mess

speckled black & gold like
                    midnight & the stars

that define its edges.
                  That there are

edges at all hurts. Shouldn't
                  the dead carry

less weight, less expectation of
                    awe?

The pages begin to fill themselves:
                    measurements, comparisons,

organs so small you're not sure

                    interiors aren't ash; like

what rests, useless & cooling, beneath

                          the fire your father

last night showed you how

                  to light, mostly

he said, so you won't keep asking

                    when your mother will return.

All the names of all the men,

especially the forgotten, are here   at our kitchen table asking
     for something they can taste. Our mouths perform

the usual rituals: tear into, grind, swallow, then recount
     exaggerated narratives of how we spent our days. We listen

for pauses long enough to interject, pivot attention our way.
     The dead have nothing to offer but stories. & names. The names

they offer could be anyone's aunts or uncles, lovers, murderers,
     children. They no longer belong   to just one

body, one inimitable life. Not that we give them the time   it takes
     to be re-remembered, mourned,   properly mourned,

which in some cultures means celebrated. We are a moving-on kind
     of people. A let sleeping dogs lie kind of people.

This house, this one room in this one house, at just this moment:
     that is our axis of orbit. Not a philosophy   but gesture.

Not a history, just ghosts. Without names. Only when I'm asking
     for forgiveness do I call the absence beside me *father.*

Scale Model of a Country at Dawn

*A Hobson's choice is a free choice in which only one thing is
offered. Because a person may refuse to accept what is offered,
the two options are taking it or taking nothing.*

Either side of a saw, either a beheaded mountain
or not enough coal to last the winter; a startled

horse beats itself against an open barn door,
imitating flight, while the hay catches fire, &

emptied of organs, painted to look less still,
my mother has never looked more herself.

Is this shoebox of Indian head nickels I've kept
since childhood more valuable sold or unspent?

If I'm passing myself down to my son, every
symptom & silence & pent-up joy, so too the rage,

this scale model of manhood. If the morning birds
ever let up, perhaps we can hear our songs rise

beyond our hearing. Like a muzzle flash
in a bright room, like another loved one

stuffed into an already ghosted house,
like the loose rocks that suggest a wall

once stood here but no longer, unless
we choose to build it, & so we build it

either to cut one property off from another
or to give us something to ruin, & celebrate.

Property Line

Sprigs from hacked-down trees catch & choke the push mower.

Bees make wide open doors of fallen peaches. Refuse to leave

like summer houseguests. I watch tanned men retire from the nearby

field, men who will sleep like heaps of kindling. Like excess hay

bales the government pays good money to burn. This too is a sign.

Entered from the wound-side of things, the world is ready

for autumn. Is made up of cycles & extinctions. Is extinct.

Our half-lit house, already dimming to night. Fireflies. Cigar smoke.

A jury of stars swells up. Bursts.

Where Astrology Ends

Thank god the stars
are not your daughters

anymore. & the wise
man chained to a stone

hacked apart, restored,
just to be eaten again

for bringing us fire
no longer looks like

your grandfather. After
twelve hours in the airless

factory your town was built
around, the way he'd carry

that fire home shares only
a passing resemblance to

the deities of old: all envy
& spite, whir & hiss, prayer-

worthy violence. How
the machinery of that world

hasn't changed so much as lost
a bit of faith in translation. Faith

that cruelty sanctioned by higher
powers is a fair trade-off for all

this living in the light. Faith that
sacrificing your youngest might

rescue drought-gutted crops.
When you pull the sky down

each night to show your ten-year-old
daughter what it means to rain,

thank god there are far fewer gods
in the name of fealty to defile her.

Nativity

To be so inhabited: immaculate
body flooded with unrequited
                              light;

virginal no longer the right word, though
still untouched by human hands;   *forced*
upon, defiled, better known as

                         miracle.

A violation of doves rises
from the blood spotting her sheets.

An uncarved block of wood
being whittled into savior.

& the sheep are growing restless.

Emancipation is the wrong word
when water breaks &   the true wailing begins.
                              Mercy, revelation. No

one is safe from the wolves   in our hearts.

The sky flints with stars men follow to praise their creation.

On This Night, or Any Other

In the dream, you lie so motionless
it's the world that walks through you.

A brokenly lit road bisects a pasture
no horses have trampled, devoured, prayed

with their whole bodies to in more years
than your father can count. Or grandfather.

But there are stories—in this dream—older
than a town's collapse. Than bruise & hand-

me-down overalls two sizes larger than anyone
could wear without falling, without a faceful of earth.

Than the sneers others pretend to hide behind
their delicate hands. Yours are calloused over & want

for something to want for. A single gesture to mean
your body is more than vessel, less than what passes for

love now. What passes for love now hurts
your knees. The denim's worn down in places,

stained in others; not by grease & grasswork, history.
In this dream you're cut to look like a boy but asked ungently

for another boy's body to enter & to remain there, wildly.
It's a holy thing, the stories say, & maybe they're right

about tomorrow's promise. You, lying there motionless under a full
weight of sky. Suffocating. Dreaming. A field, naked but for all

                              the horses you dream there.

Appaloosa

Nothing spooks the horses into flight
like inertia. Not lightning, barn fire.

Not the whips we take to their sides

to drive them forward. There's always
room for a bit more suffering, right?

But something profound happens,
mid-field, multi-colored living field,
when the fences hold & the light steadies.

Calm, unusable day leaves nothing for night
                                        to undo.

Like my brother so utterly broken by
our unbroken world, carving escape
tunnels into his veins, breaking into
our house to steal what he already owns.

Like my ten-year-old body burrowing
beneath a fence six inches from the gate.

Like my mother, staring out the kitchen
window all day, cleaning the last crumbs
of her dreams from our plates.

Like the horses, seduced closer to our open
palms with carrots & promises: that someday

we will wild them again, beat & break them…
                                        anything.

Prayer for the Boy Lost Inside the Boy

I'll see you among the cruel things
winter chases south or hibernates

& in the particular cruelties winter
invites into our limbs & lungs.

The earth's always too soft or callous
to leave the buried be. Shovel-snap,

slippage. But never an enduring
silence. I'll see you in the shadow-

play sparrows paint up & down
the bedroom wall, in that partially

illuminated movement just outside
candle reach. & for when there isn't

such a soft darkness in the house,
I'll see you in the endless vigils kids

keep locked inside so the world won't
see they haven't given up yet. Maybe

I'll see you in their giving up too.
This is how I bathe my dead:

with a pumice stone & words
that mean less & less the louder

I speak them. I don't think I mean
a damn thing I've ever said above

a whisper. That's why I speak in wails
& roars, why I see the whole or nothing

at all—my face in all faces, in yours, vice versa.
I know it's just a matter of time before I stop

seeing what I need to see in whatever is kind
enough to lend me its image. The kindest

thing about being human is that everything
gifts us its image—for a moment or forever.

As It Is on Earth

It's like that sometimes. A man bends
so completely he begins believing in
his own holiness. An empty house
kids are too scared to vandalize sees itself
in time as haunted. Even the moon
our dogs wail to each night as if in prayer
fears a response is expected. The war
my brother brought home & the home he
pined for in war converge in an unruly
absence. Is it finally fair to say like gods
we make images to pour ourselves into?
Like rivers, how they tend to move
farther from the source? What skin
remembers & the mind reimagines:

between them a truth serrated as light.

Larynx

All this hum must come from somewhere.

If not intent, at least origin // at least a throat
greenly opening to spring or exhausted elms

hunkering down so the winds won't break them
as they have so many others // at least belief:

the world is worth singing into, that echoes

collect in the corners like spiderless webs,
their silken strings still trembling with past

prey // at least, like angels & their wretched call,
there is an elsewhere our voices are meant

to grow toward; in this caged forest air

bodies throw themselves into the bars
with the wild rapture of being heard

for once, as if these countless centuries
can be healed in a single act. It would be good

// at least to call the steady static within

a bridge & listening a shore & adding to it
current // at least to say there is a yes

rising in our throats, drowning out the wail
of us, repronouncing our truth // carrying it.

Some of What Sings

Last season's boats percuss against the dock.
The wind makes chimes of their hollows,
arias of winter's birdlessness. Gutted,

our hunger synchs with a prow's nothing-
to-cut-through groans. We have nothing left
to catch & release or conquer & devour.

Going slack then taut, slack // taut, the ropes
seem to be holding. Held together by
the tensile strength of our own narrative,

we are singing *this is home* into conchs
& into the ears of the dead, harmonizing
the sea with the bodies we export across it.

Conch

I admire the hollow, the keeping-things-
in. Even after the sea has coughed it up,
how it never stops ringing with home.

In the whirl & whorl of it all, a small
note taped to the inside of my heart:
remember, there is always something

to forgive, to be forgiven for. How
smoothly the past bleeds into now.
On my sleeve, the faded white

farmhouse I take to burning
each night in my mind. Everyone
I've ever loved inside. The tide,

as it inches in, swallowing sand & all
my brief castles. & a shell so sonorous
I almost forget its missing body.

Our Pasts, Like Lighthouses

Today you will write about lights
— Langston Hughes

I saw the sign
scuffed & hooked
over a boarded-up
doorframe, freed
from meaning
only *open* or *closed,*
doctor or *butcher,*
just a beautifully
blank face gone
all impartial & true.
Each brick-shattered
window its own
cathedral. Eye. Finally,
with history holstered,
the barrel but lukewarm,
the fossils of fallen stars
have a chance to shine
again, to be dusted off
& to dust our future
ancestors. My daughter,
for example.
How little her skin
resembles mine. How
if this were 1944, she
and her brother would be
(dis)placed in *Minidoka*
or *Manzanar. Harmony.*
Harmony; how she loves
to say that word without
the weight of context.
How like a lighthouse

she scans every god-
damn corner of her
safe little sea in search
of some wreck to save.
To guide back into harbor.
Today, it's my heart. *Love,*
thank you for that. & for this
rotted old wooden sign briefly
we will leave our names on.

❦

SUTURE

❦

All We Ever Wanted Was Everything[1]

We weren't so hungry our gods
could be eaten. Even with wine.
Mouthfuls of ash. Not yet. It takes
more than a house in disrepair
to imagine the nails will hammer
themselves, more than a few years
of darkness to demand so much of light.
But we were hungry. For something.
A country to take with us long after
we shunned it. A barrel fire to last the night.
A word for salve that didn't imply injury.
Some whiskey. Brown bread. Cigarettes. Stars
we could see well into morning. It's not
the illness that kills you, my grandfather
would say, but giving up on a cure.
That was before the illness killed him,
back when you & I were small & small
our cruelties. Those holes the moon cleaves
through the clouds look a bit too much like
exit wounds now. & the stars, shell casings
left to cool in a field. A wilderness of neon,
pigeons, prayers, silence. As if we're hungry
for a light to reach us down here, frayed
like the end of a snapped rope.

---

1 This title is inspired by the song of the same name by Bauhaus.

Everywhere is the same

half-acre of Montana sky
burning,

the same erratic birds without a firmament   to rise toward,

hills whose shade refuses to lengthen, comfort. All the animals in us
scattering

for the cover of bars & churches, their gods
one in the same,   making melodies of crisis.

I would feed you my body

if it parted the smoke for just one night. One dawn that wakes
without hunger & cough.
Like that wafer that stands in for deliverance, the wine meant to taste
like blood
& does.

I would give you
my voice, my lungs, the whole damn thing
to scream from
if the wind could carry it
out over the field.

If echo had an aftermath. Like fire. Like this fire we've lit:

swallowing & spitting back up: charred, changed. Not a prayer,
exactly, but something

like asking without expecting an answer.   I would return you
to the safety we say we remember from childhood

if that country still existed in us.

Sinkholes

The earth we assumed

would still be there in the morning has hollowed
                        into a field of mouths

stinking of Grandpa's   day-old whiskey breath.

            Everything time has hardened

chaps & splits like migrant hands   & all the lights

we left on in the house to remind the world we are still
                        a part of it

        blow out together.

Wastewater drowns the rhododendrons. What's passed
through our systems bubble up to the surface as mud,

the kind of mud they say man was shaped from
into whatever it is we are now.   I remember

when men were sturdier, Grandpa says, & women kept
                    the garden green.

I remember when holes   were made to be filled.
I remember when holes could be filled with prayer

        & our bodies stretched heavy over them.

Solar Retinopathy

Eyes bleached by the sun, by staring
so long there is no sky anymore // no

light // no feathered bodies carving up
the light, humanizing it // just a field

without enough contrast to call it white /
/ as when death creeps into the bones

it's hard to recognize those last days
as life // why holding the love of seeing

too tight can erase both // have we chosen
the wrong thing to love or the wrong way

to love it // with knees bent at the prescribed
angle in this tall tall grass in such burning

brightness, how we struggle against ourselves
to find something more to witness

Self-Portrait as Travelogue

Say she's the blur
            of a passing landscape.

The lack of *here*
when the road just keeps
            going regardless.

A fistful of tangled   wool blown free
            into a barbed fence.

One of so many mile markers no one reads
            except when broken
            down & awaiting rescue.

Say, in the years since she left us, the heart
   has made a weapon of forgetting,

that the sky speaks   its lightning quieter now,
       that the sky blushes sunset when we ask
            for a bit more time.

But for this, the horizon we're driving off into would scream
            forever.

Say it's okay to assume love
            will still be there

when we enter the next town   then the next,
that all dirt roads lead to highway which lead to the sea.

Say the sea & say it like you mean it. Trace her face
            on the rain-   vagued window.

Over the radio's delicate static, repeat the names of the dead
            until they hurt again.

Ministry

Ash burns a small star into her small forehead
as the real ones above she once shaped into myths
scatter in all this smoke. If there is a difference

between wildfire & prayer, my daughter is too young
to speak it. & I am too old. Zephyr or exit wound—if
there's a difference. Mouths filled with dust or all those

no longer pronounceable songs. Tonight, the god
of this porch is a wounded sunset. An uncalm absence
of larks. Our hands crumbled together for warmth. Sustenance.

To ready the night for us, I am driving nails into palmless
boards. Into an x or cross—if there's still a difference, let's
bless the chaff & wheat alike. The named bodies. & nameless.

The forests we water & forests we cannot stop burning.

Apiary & Woodshop

I can't remember which saint burned
herself pure & which the Romans

burned the impurities from or if it matters
sacrifice vs. sparrow,

natural or forced flight.
Where a bridge collapses,

shores remain. When the shores yield,
cliffs. If the cliffs,

we'll still find something
high to fall from. Here

is a half-finished city shining
like the last untainted image of heaven:

crane rusted in place,
mid-air, useless, a painting

of an angel descending toward
a miracle that never comes.

Here the hinges of a house scream
from disuse. Do we even have

the right equipment to tune this
bedlam of bees into a honeyed song?

Will we always be three boards from
finishing this little boat?

Coat of Bees

For a long time, the stingers we left
          unplucked from our naked thighs
bristled & barbed when together our bodies broke
                              in the uncut field, falling
& rising back up from, intersecting like

               roofline & sky, like christless
timber — a doe & her two fawns
          craned over a tepid brook drinking
up evening in fits & swallows nervously eyeing

your cresting spine, the wounds swelling our skin
                    red & wild, that nothing-

to-do-but-fuck-it-all of a youth spent
          wearing the world like a woolen hand-
me-down coat, scratching ourselves raw, poking
                    each hive, daring hurt to hurt,

praying the doe eventually forgets us, her children go
          unscarred, that our mothers will move on
                              to better children,

          finally; in an orgasm
that quivered our bodies like fevered acuity —
          another first of so many derelict firsts, gone before
                    we thought to ask what it meant —

Community Service

We are standing beside what used to be a river
twenty or thirty years ago & fishing from it
crushed cans & other unshatterable things
as penance. The old highway still rumbles
occasionally above us, shedding its glass
& plastic skin, but the hard part is praying
to be made of that same permanence. Nothing
here leaves on its own. Discolors, only
wilts at the name; structures intact. What
had no agency still has no agency & with it
no death. I don't remember the name of the man
I hurt. I don't remember the label of the bottle,
only that tapped on a table it made good teeth.
I don't remember exactly when we stopped
calling this a river. With the last fish caught?
When it could no longer hush a cigarette's glow?
Beneath the new highway a few miles over
there are currents & eddies, thirsty animals,
men who've done worse with their lives
scavenging the depths with nets for the same
forgiveness. Everywhere the same wild
grasses sway like tiny houses on fire.

Open Season

Rifle crack.
Silence.
All this god-forsaken waiting

to see what falls.

Sometimes a bird or two. Or stars. Sometimes

a brother's son who refuses the brightly
glowing vest because it seems too *girly*.

We're all trying to prove
ourselves to someone.

Today we're hoisting a buck up into a flatbed
as prayer.

As prayer, we're thrusting our hands deep into it.
& bone knives.

In a field still stained in moonlight
waking

silently to color,

three days before the season opens
to blood & gristle,

we're here

to take what we can in our mouths
                         & chew.

Before the animals ready for flight.
Before others taint the land with their prayers.

Winter Bazaar

Not-yet broken crockery.

Sky, for the moment, intact.

A table heavies with glass-
blown angels bent
at the wing into prayer.

Nothing worth note
to forgive this morning.

So many bearded faces
stack lengthwise over
matching plastic crosses.

Someone's grandmother
praises the transcendence
of Marionberry & cinnamon.

Your mother & mine covet
the same ceramic dish
that captures a couple
before their fall.

Naked & unashamed,
birch quiver all around us in ecstasy.

Huge hands cover my eyes,

guide me blindly out
onto the sidewalk where all

the children are busy
fashioning their fathers
from gray trampled snow.

Backyard Hymnal

O the church of it. Rope
snapped from the high
branches like silenced
organ chords, tire just lying
there keeping the grass
from rebirth. Stairs rusted
off the slide. A rumor of
smoke works its way skyward
from an anthill. Our bodies
ride hobbyhorses fashioned
from broomsticks & the heads
of our sisters' plush pets. Off
in the near distance, chainsaws
chew through dawn after dawn
until our fathers return
with a winter's worth of birch,
spruce, pine. Softer woods burn
hungrily, with earnest. None of that
slow steady buildup to warmth.
We want the world now, its teeth.
We want to remain eternal
for a few more years. Now
that your mother is dead & mine
can't keep her hands off that
yard sale cross & the blade of Grandpa's
WWII penknife has broken off leaving us
with nothing to autograph the barn with
but our fists & such pure love
of this place it would be unholy not to
strike match to straw to see
how bright we can make it.

Portrait of a Portrait on Fire

with my eyes closed this long
i almost forget how his face
blistered & bruised from a canvas
we'd unhung from the living
room wall & dragged across
a wilded lawn to let burn
by itself beneath the same heavy
sky he in turn praised & blamed
& the cherry trees gnarled & knuckled
overhead casting shadows too long
to escape though in our trying
to love just this one violent gesture
the kind of salve immolation implies
when the unlit face of night refuses
to hurt as it should as if absence
anchors us together a family briefly
holding & being held by an ecstatic
prayer-like silence pierced by spark
& ash our hands linked for this one
night not at all like a barbed metal fence

Leave No Trace

Sometimes the ash from the fires
that keep night from our bones
must be swept clean & the earth

returned to itself.

Sometimes we must gather up
our shattered glasses & stars
with both hands like children
& cradle them safely home.

All this living is nothing
if what we've burned lingers

into dawn. So all this
living ends up nothing
more often than not.

Still I can't bring myself
to take down the pictures
of the dead I carry inside

or reseed the patches
of field I've worn
down with my body.

I'm sorry, Mom.

I'm sorry trees
I've knifed my initials into
& crudely carved hearts.

I'm sorry, birds,

not for pulling you
ungently from the sky
but for leaving you
in this burning summer grass

uneaten.

We Carry Wildfires in Our Guts

The Carr Fire raging in Northern California is so large and
hot that it is creating its own localized weather system
— CNN, July 31, 2018

As a fish market in summer.
As a church choking
on its own incense.
The air here is heavy
as a long line of men
churning like pistons
smoking whatever fits
between their lips waiting
for a bar to go neon at night.
As if our hands weren't
always feeding furnaces.
As if we're not living
in one of many discarded
rough drafts of heaven.
As if we ever believed
the sky breathable, lit
from above, that when
the clouds part briefly
something other than
tinder would fall.

In the Language of Drought

Whole legions of them. Pronghorns. Mule deer. A wildness
of insects. All fleeing our dried-out riverbeds. The opposite
of a nursery book. Life broken down to saliva & swallow.
A line read of Steinbeck minus the rabbits. There's an ecstasy
to absence. A palpable pleasure in wants finally succumbing
to needs. It's good to need things again. Taken back to basics:
the sun, blacked & blued, a body dragged kicking & praying
across its sky. The sky on fire. The prairie grass is a pilot light.
My mother, still ash. If thirst is a currency, let's spend all this
on wax horses with wicks growing from their heads. Melting
mountains. Frantic horizon. Javelina. Meadowlark. The water
jugs we stored in the storm cellar for times like these. Everything
that has sung its song, beautifully, & left us deliberate ascetics.

Oasis

A sudden lushness

sprung from a single desert rain
already swimming in locusts.

Naked, in the briefly raging
river, absent its skin, a pulled-apart

body, thousands of bodies preparing
to take its place.

A blanket for its dying. A corset. Flame.

That we are here watching the all-or-nothing
of that flame, hungry as ever, terrified;

a blessing

light as gunpowder, sparking,
as light itself before the heat takes hold.

Zoo Animals

Plume: as in that bright precious
feathered thing my children once

loved from behind its wiry fence,
the lack to touch equating over time

to intimacy; as in the intimacy of distant
factories staining the clouds yellow

like cigarette smoke or prayers, either
really, once the room's become a vessel for

ghosts; as in preening myself before
the mirror of my son's eyes, demanding

so much more than I can even pretend
to offer, how we play at goodbyeing

the world every kiss, every finger-lock,
every song, elegy, orison—borrowed or

stolen; as in covering the whole house
with a tarp of brilliantly serrated light

& saying the rest is darkness, is cage,
saying I'm a different animal than the one

                they once loved, zealously, from afar.

Fever

When you hold your child's body like this,
cold as unexcavated earth, wet with want,

making oaths to anything that will listen, *please*
and *god* and the usual silences, so much useless

splendor cradled fetally between raw open hands.
When the field just keeps going without you. Or

so you're told. When anatomies collude with night.
Dark steepled night. When you're reminded it's all

just machinery, rusting, this shame not a halo taken
off once the breathing steadies, again. And again,

when that something of the stars still in us blinks
in and out of existence. (Dis)placed cathedrals.

Gut-shot worship. This bittering. When, disordered,
your heart is that rarely seen bird no one knows

how to name. Will it mourn or devour its young?
Congregate a nest from healthy or broken

limbs? When lowering that tiny trembling body
down to its ill-kept bed, studded in plush and perfect

need. This early hour before the world wakes up.
When rubbing your hands together just might spark

the required warmth. A song returning. On the wind,
birdsong and wail. The field extends. The shame intact.

Sycamores

Dying two hundred times
with as many rebirths
sounds like a lot of work;

papering the earth red
without so much as a war,
no sacrifice, tears, eulogy.

& never the same sparrows,
never knowing more than
a season or two the living

bodies born in your arms.
Remember how terrified
we were those long sleepless

nights huddled over cribs
waiting for the absence of child
to overtake us again?

What silence implies in a world
defined by wail. Remember when
we delivered your mother's ashes

to the brook & how long it took
to look at water the same way?
If only our children were trees

we could watch them ghost
all winter — shiver whitely, leafless,
barely breathing — without all these

terrible prayers. We could celebrate
how light returns as swiftly & forever
as when it left us.

Echolocation

The forest is darker than the darkness around stars.
To organize things back into shapes & faces, we listen
for where one body ends & another begins. We estimate

                    & assume. We hope

tracking disembodied voices will someday spell out
the name of the country we've lost & forgive
us its trespass. That any animal can see like this!

                Can map the world by its wail.

But who needs eyes or hands when everything is burning
darker than a rekindled cross, so dark it's impossible
to tell one shadow from another; what could be a ghost

        or predator or prey calling us back
        to a home we've never left.

Suture

Until it no longer held,   the bridge was eternal.

& even after its dissolution
                into the concept of a bridge,

into stories handed down generations
of how once there was a way
                                across,

we say we can taste the rust
                        & hear

(when the river shuts up for a night)

the feet of children
                        (who must be long dead
                                    by now)
                stampeding barefoot across it.

They sound like matches dropped in water.

They sound like parables
                told so often we confuse them
                                        with memories.

When the water is clear enough to see the bottom,
we say we can see the bottom. We fish it for ruin
                & come up empty-handed. Tonight

the whole town is coming together (again) to discuss rebuilding

a bridge no one remembers having ever been there

(but must have, once,

if we're to call the other side

a shore).

⊜

Object Permanence

⊜

The Gospel According to Here

Where the edges of homes run together
an incision of alley just wide enough

for bodies to pass without scraping
the paint off the bricks. A flowerless

plot of raised earth meant for greener
things. If those are strays praying wildly

with their teeth, it's not to the moon.
I don't think we'd recognize that god

anymore. The sky's strung with LED
lights, held together by cords we un-

plug to bring us closer to night.
In other rooms, men & women &

children & love being made as
efficiently as possible before

limbs untangle into fists. Shattered
dishes. Ghosts waiting to be born.

From other rooms, the delicate scent
of cardamom & patience. Of someday.

& such a splendid contrast of flags
duct taped to every window

sealing up the cracks, keeping
most of our heat inside.

Parallax

Headlight-brightened bodies pass
                    by, briefly, before blackening
                    again in the nameless expanse of gulch
                    & grass. One could almost say

          illusion, that all this seeing
          is a trick the light plays to keep us

                    rooted in place. In this case,
                    driver, subject. If things worked out

differently, we'd be out there wandering the object-heavy night

                    dreaming that our raised thumbs meant
          you can trust me & unarmed, then drinking
          the moon from crushed cans rusting by the road.

                    At 60 miles per hour, the world seems
                    such a tender thing, the chorus sustainable,
                    all this darkness an excuse to call our parents

          & pledge we haven't failed them yet. As one does
          a country or a god. Winterbare,

a tree blurs by like someone else's skeleton. The landscape moves
                    uninjured by frost. From here

          I can love generously, believe

what passes is just some earlier version of heaven.

Forever Daylight

Again the sun fails to dissolve & I
cannot wash the light from your hair.

The world stands excruciatingly visible,
stuck in its song. What the night must steal

to give us something to rediscover
about ourselves never leaves our hands.

No gauzy horizon. No ambiguity. Nothing
to unlearn. We draw the curtains. But even this

is a candle. Even the bent heads of icecaps
melting. The fjord rising. These sheep are not

the dreaming kind. Rugged, furious, walking
cliff sides as if water. That something can have

no gods at all & still be holy. That we are finally
seeing ourselves in the full light of another's

eyes & cannot stop flinching. Our throats gone
gravel & road salt from all this ceaseless awe.

Square Dance at Dusk

Not golden. More the off-yellow of old rust.
                             It's easy to say it's the sky

adopting the color of the hay on the floor & the bleached streaks
                                      in her hair

          & that everything is at heart a mockingbird.

This fiddle could be any fiddle. These bodies move like bodies.
It's been this way for four hundred years; this furor

          of limbs, carefully chosen steps
             toward & away from thrall,

     bourbon & boarded up mills, the world leaning on tired stars.

          At this time of night, well before the loving
                 has begun, the windows
            are full of staring crows.

          The unlit face of the moon is as bright as the true.

If there's a difference between unjoining & reuniting, I hope
                             we never learn it.

Reading *Ozymandias* in Astoria

Beneath these storm-shaped trees, bent inland,
hammocking the glassy shards of light so none
strike us, at least not enough to illuminate or hurt,
we're rubbing sticks together in hopes of a fire
that'll last the night. The only fires we've known
to catch & stay & eventually, briefly, warm us
others have lit. It's the same with snow, how it
only hardens what's never been particularly soft.
Or the kinds of walls worthy of pilgrimage. Or wars
without end. To unpack someone else's history & make it
our own is the easy part. But what we burn never
remains relevant after its ash cools &, taken by
the wind, moves on. That *we're still out here trying*
should count for something doesn't slake our thirst
or satisfy the gods our ancestors placed in our hands,
delicately, so not to be broken, like glass beads
traded, duplicitously, with natives for an island.
Irreparable: that's the kind of breaking we're after;
a fire so persuasive our grandchildren will pray to it.

Controlled Burn

Acre after acre left unburnt.
Full families of wolves gone
unshot. & the chickens we keep
to teach our children where meat
comes from are getting nervous.
The wire-thin pen cannot stop
the world from entering. Like how
quitting cigarettes only delays
a mother's cancer. Like all those
desperate prayers that refuse
to restrain night. Like a country
sealed off by concrete & barbs.
There are just too many stars
to snuff out in one lifetime,
too many gaps in the parapet.
I walk my son & daughter out
into the wild unburnt green
every morning, holding their hands
like weapons, & ask the world
if I'm doing this right. This living.
This trying too hard to make beautiful.

Interlude

One crow, then another. Soon
the lines that light our houses
will snap under feather & caw.

Our little empires gone dark
& without the TV: oarless, windless.

& I don't know if my son will still
recognize me in him anymore.

What's weightless on its own
burdens en masse. Not that

we need to be told the whole
damn thing relies on façade.

We all have mirrors & heavy
curtains to cover up the mirrors,

strangers within rock-throwing
distance from our houses to call
neighbor, godparent, rival.

The staples that hold her belly together
imply rupture as much as birth.

When our power returns, will we
even remember its absence? More

blue glow & scripted stories. Well-lit
kitchen. Dinner & dessert & again.
Crows moved on to the eaves.

This brittle little body in my arms
I still cannot make a temple.

Wide as a Heaven Hemmed in by Hills

Some blood still in it. Some yeast to make bread from a body;
some bones not quite ground down enough to swallow. Still,
some solace when the mice chew through the rafters & open
the sky to our song. Sometimes it is like this. Veined with light,
a white clapboard church choked in vines & your parents
somewhere in it doing whatever the dead do to stay lit. Some
things will be just where you left them. When you come back,
the same mountain mined beyond repair & the same lack
of children in the park. Just dogs. Nooses remade into tire swings.
Home; all the same hungers. The sky still giving little slack.
& those old paper prayers from childhood snagged on the same
branches. Some birds with all the flight knocked out of them still
thrashing at the air trying to ascend.

Canaveral

Some things are damned to flare up before breaching

the surface of space, umbilical smoke as it continues

the trajectory, like a giant white Kanji character

brushed onto the air, like a parasite projected

from its microscopic plate against the heavens,

one after another mother covering her child's

wet & widening eyes. Tendrils of doubt, notes

jotted into the margins of how the world really works.

When you stop making lists of *why*, the reasons distill,

refine, & are pure. That we will do it all again, repetition

as worship, as eventually adding up to something; above

this one is another sky shot full of holes.

Genesis

That in the beginning nothing was
known of the beginning only explains
so much. That our fathers had fathers
who traced their trembling back
to strange sources. Rain as weeping.
Storm: rage. All the suffering
wrapped up in us: deserved. & the awe,
the rinds of light that make their way
down here, burning like an anthem.

When the sky can't fill it all in, I too
color outside the edges. Isn't that what
edges are for? Like rules, how they say
you must master before breaking them.
Like how the field is only filled with
what we can see in the field. Doe tracks.
Wolf tracks. Waiting. So much waiting for
our turn. Everything burning endlessly
with the odor of its birth.

Sediment

As dying rivers go, the one they say carries us
like branch-woven baskets into the waiting
hands of a greater current isn't so bad. Those
I remember from childhood tended to steer
our little paper boats sealed with beeswax—
as if that meant waterproof, as if there were no
such thing as sink or swallow—toward storm
drains & the toothy clowns that live in them.
A few years later, after swapping monsters
for whiskey & matches, sex or what rightly
should be called attempts, the rivers seemed
drunk on former glories, like gods returned
to earth to find belief only goes one way.
Have the myths changed that much or simply
our listening? Arroyo. Wash. Dried-out gulch
shaped by eons to fit our burgeoning fires;
the same flame that drove our ancestors west
& begged Odysseus home. Let's follow this
arid crust of clay & scrub as far as its story
takes us. They say there's an ocean out there
somewhere. Eternity & gulls. Undertows. Calm.
A kind of drowning we can learn to breathe.

Bifurcation

God enters through the wound.
— Carl Jung

How a river is made to split
to irrigate far-off fields.

How a child breaks
over knee after knee

to teach him something
about tomorrow. Perhaps

I really am only bare feet
muddying my father's house,

the frailest fork of a once-
mighty waterway. Still

there's comfort in the distance
between real & imagined burdens,

where I refuse to bend & where
I have been made to, that cross

he carries bitterly in his mouth
& the hand-me-down one on our backs.

Aperture

I know the hinges give me away. To be this open
requires doors. Night-sealed, dead-bolted, rusted,

shedding blood-colored dust. Roughly the size of
the world, the world that enters is sweet as a head

of foam scraped off a teacup, unforgiving as an Old
Testament story. The god I used to think I was loved

pain. Distance. & starlings. He'd dare his bike faster
down unpaved paths & relish the fall. Show the scars

off to everyone at school. Invent entire mythologies
to explain the stars, where they go in winter. Where

my mother went. Silent house. & frostbite.
                                        The rest

was just a parable. A paraffin river. Holy. It's simple
enough: where there is no memory, nothing happened.

So, nothing that happened hurt. I'm not sure what
changed, but these days the doorframe shudders &

yields in certain weathers. The fence posts I had
hammered down so damn hard loosen. Then

they give too. An empty house testifies to everything
it once held. Held or holding? Both in- & egress.

The whole I'm told we return to

eventually, // unyoked from wire & // weed, muted to a noun that no
longer // wilds violently // against its box, like horses sleeping
through a barn fire, // like a fire that blackens not // a single rafter or
the dreams of // horses sleeping inside, the words we boys // hurt
ourselves on grating // smaller boys over & the barbed // fences
meant to keep us // from our neighbor's // daughters, that nothing-
quite-sticks of a mother's // tired prayers, // her light amputated by
heavy // curtains, cottonwood, & an absent // father, bold neon bars
& the distance // a body must travel to see itself // beautiful, to see //
the beauty the field buries beneath // months of hardened snows:

gone; now,

the lanterns born into // my eyes, long cold // relit not anything like
cigarette-sparked hay bundled into barn // fire keeping // the horses
from dreaming far // from our halters; eventually // it's all the same
silent // congregation of cormorants, // they keep telling me, // that
one enormous world- // swallowing *we* // all of us together again
without // bodies eating // without food holding you // without arms

American Bounty

Water the color of stripped copper wires—the kind we sell for
                                        pennies at the local scrapyard,
the kind we must ruin a house for—
                                        works its way down our bodies.

We are draining what we can from the world, saving the rest
                        for when the rains end. We're told

heaven can't splinter & seep forever. We're told we are lucky to live
    in a kind of heart-   land where one thirst replaces another.

                    As if answering our prayer,

the rusty tin barrel in the front yard, wide as a still-believed-in
                    sky, just keeps refilling with storm.

Restoration

In the absence of repair, I'll make due
with telling my children this failing house
& the country we planted it in & the world
that refuses to stop blooming all around us

& the stars can be shelter enough. Like freckles,
the soft spots in the walls are just surface stains.
Like the sky, roofs are meant to leak, bow.
& replacing the buckets every night is a ritual

akin to prayer. For every power outage, a use
for candles. For every cricket living in the walls
grating one leg against another, a song to help us
sleep. In their silence, the dead are invincible;

I'll tell my children it takes that much time
to learn to listen. I'm still learning what not
to say about the bell-jarred caterpillars they keep
expecting to break into butterflies.

The Confession

Forgive me this small box of synonyms
                    borrowed from older tongues.

& forget the telephone game we played last night
                    when only my voice carried, intact.

That there are no rules to it all, just instinct & mistranslation &
     loving our slice of the world, by which I mean where *trespass*

confuses with *own*. That none of the bones the river coughs up
          are mine. Never mind that heights are measured in
                              hands & distance

by the chasm between hand & reached-for star. There's no room for
                    stars here.
No barbed fence someone hasn't raked herself over so her son can
                                   live

that much closer to hope, shelter. Forgive me the bullet
          a stranger lodged in your language, that when I say the body

I mean it abstractly. Show me the heart a mother must eat so her son
          won't suffer our tomorrows. Plant it in my hands. Let's agree

something should grow there. Let's pass *should* around this circle of
          ears & mouths & see if it changes in the end. Never mind

that it always changes in the end. Forgive me the stars I don't have
          to reach for. These bones that still aren't mine. & the box.

                    This small box.

Salinas

Miles pass. Breaths. Landscapes scorch
by the window. Upturned faces everywhere

hunting for rain. Lettuce, wild vines, insects
                & the things that eat them. Undocumented

                  work going on in the deepest
                     recesses of summer.

The smell of machines, ungreased levers
working each other up into whine.

A horse on the horizon. A jangle of belled goats. Thirst.

                       Hands, their splitting.

               Our headlights stay on all day
                      to remind us to see.

Nothing says *stay.*
Nothing has to.

           We are pulled in too many directions
             to make a home of things.

Proof that we were ever here is already disappearing.

Object Permanence

Everything's still here;
even after hidden behind
the world's back, stolen
from view, presumably
erased from existence,
like a loved one you have
no photograph to grieve,
like that red wagon my
father broke & scrapped
& said I'd only imagined
dragging through our garden
which once—& therefore still—
throbbed the morning green.
If leaving infancy behind has
taught me anything, it's never
assume the disappeared cannot
return. If what I've lost
over the years is a lesson,
it's that nothing returns
in its original form. See,
my mother would say,
how the pale blue ball
I've thrown up into the sky
is now a moon; gorgeously
unattainable. See me like that.

Being Islands

Petrels drag along the surface like daggers
or walk it like fragile gray Christs, depending.

The old beached shipwreck our children
climb through either speaks for the sea

or for the fingerprints we're leaving
all over it. Being islands, we have no idea

if the terrible grinding beneath us might
eventually swallow what it raised

or if our tiny bit of land lost within so much
blue will endure the next storm. Is that

why the promises our children deserve
dissolve on our tongues like salt

or poison or both? Depending
on the stars' alignment, tonight

we'll own what we've done
or none of it was ever ours.